WHO WOULD WIN?

TARANTULA

VS.

SCORPION

BY
JERRY PALLOTTA

ILLUSTRATED BY
ROB BOLSTER

Scholastic Inc.

New York   Toronto   London   Auckland
Sydney   Mexico City   New Delhi   Hong Kong

The publisher would like to thank the following for their
kind permission to use their photographs in this book:

Page 16: © Tom McHugh / Photo Researchers, Inc.; page 17: © Andres Morya Hinojosa /
DanitaDelimont.com; page 18: © Radius Images / Alamy; page 19: © Sherwin / epa / Corbis;
page 22: © Nils Jorgensen / Rex USA; page 23: top: © David M. Dennis / Animals Animals-
Earth Scenes; bottom: © McClatchy-Tribune via Getty Images

Dedicated to Pat Perry, Pat Barr, Mary Perdew, and Deanna Hill.
—J.P.
Thank you to John Singer Sargent.
—R.B.

ISBN 978-0-545-30172-5

66 65   24 25/0

Printed in the U.S.A.   40
First printing, January 2012

What would happen if a tarantula met a scorpion?
What if they were both in a bad mood and had a fight?
Who do you think would win?

SCIENTIFIC NAME OF
TARANTULA:
"Theraphosa blondi"

Meet the tarantula. There are almost 900 species of tarantulas. In this book, we will feature the largest, the goliath birdeater tarantula.

Tarantulas are hairy spiders. Spiders have four pairs of legs. Spiders are in a group of invertebrates called arachnids.

SCIENTIFIC NAME OF SCORPION:
"Leiurus quinquestriatus"

Meet the scorpion. There are more than 1,500 known species of scorpion. We will use the death stalker scorpion in our battle.

CAREFUL!

You do NOT want to get stung by a scorpion.

FACT
The largest scorpion is the emperor scorpion, which is 8 inches long. The death stalker scorpion is 3 inches long.

Scorpions are also arachnids. They have two claws and an extended tail. The scorpion has a stinger on the end of its tail. Next to the stinger is the telson, which is filled with poison.

5

TARANTULA'S BURROW

Many tarantulas live in burrows. They usually dig their own tunnel and then leave a web at the entrance to stop intruders and water from coming in. Sometimes a tarantula will move into an abandoned burrow of a snake or mouse.

Tarantula's territory

DEFINITION

A burrow is a hole or tunnel in the ground dug by an animal for a place to live.

SCORPION'S BURROW

Scorpions live under rocks, under branches, and just about anywhere they can safely hide. Most scorpions hide during the day and come out at night.

FREEZING-COLD FACT
Scorpions and tarantulas do not live in Antarctica.

Scorpion's territory

TARANTULA ANATOMY

Notice the segmented body, which is divided into two parts. The legs come out of the front part, the thorax. The back part is the abdomen.

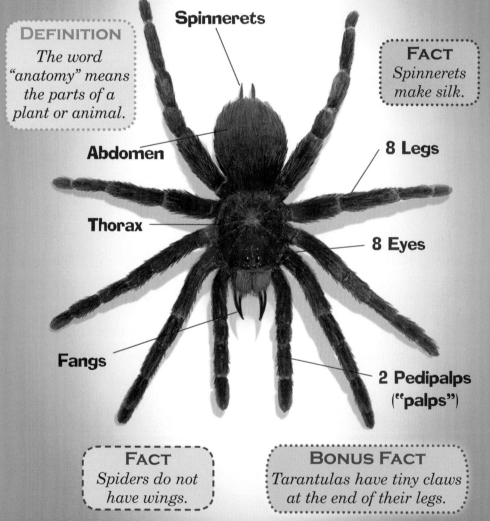

Spinnerets

FACT
Spinnerets make silk.

Abdomen

8 Legs

Thorax

8 Eyes

Fangs

2 Pedipalps ("palps")

FACT
Spiders do not have wings.

BONUS FACT
Tarantulas have tiny claws at the end of their legs.

It looks like tarantulas have ten legs, but they don't. The two legs beside their mouths are called palps. They are like arms. They help the tarantula move their food around.

SCORPION ANATOMY

Scorpions have two eyes on the top of their thorax and three to five pairs of eyes on the sides. The side eyes are called lateral eyes.

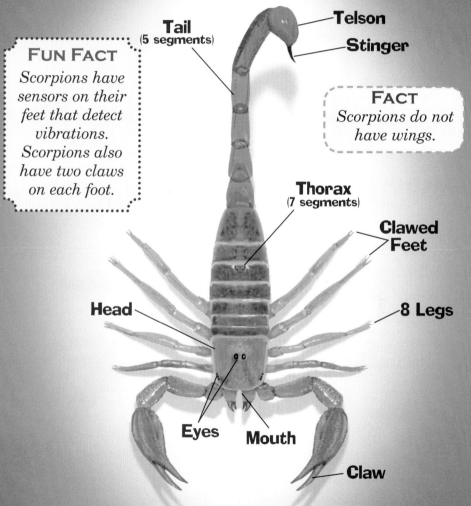

FUN FACT
Scorpions have sensors on their feet that detect vibrations. Scorpions also have two claws on each foot.

Tail
(5 segments)

Telson

Stinger

FACT
Scorpions do not have wings.

Thorax
(7 segments)

Clawed Feet

Head

8 Legs

Eyes

Mouth

Claw

DID YOU KNOW?
Arachnids do not have antennae.

GLOWING FACT
Scorpions glow under black light because they reflect ultraviolet rays.

TARANTULA WEAPONS

The tarantula's mouth has quite a bite. It carries poison in its fangs.

BOTTOM VIEW

FANGS

MOUTH

YIKES! DISGUSTING!
Tarantulas throw up digestive juices onto their prey.

Tarantulas rub their legs against their hairy bodies and shoot hair at their attackers. This is called urticating. It is a nasty weapon that makes some animals cough and have trouble breathing.

SCORPION WEAPONS

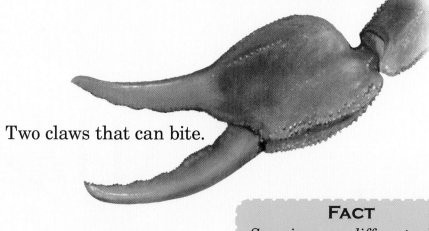

Two claws that can bite.

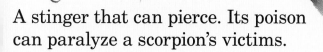

A stinger that can pierce. Its poison can paralyze a scorpion's victims.

The scorpion has two little pinchers in its mouth.

TARANTULA COUSINS?

Some animals are similar to a tarantula. Many other creatures in the animal kingdom also have eight legs.

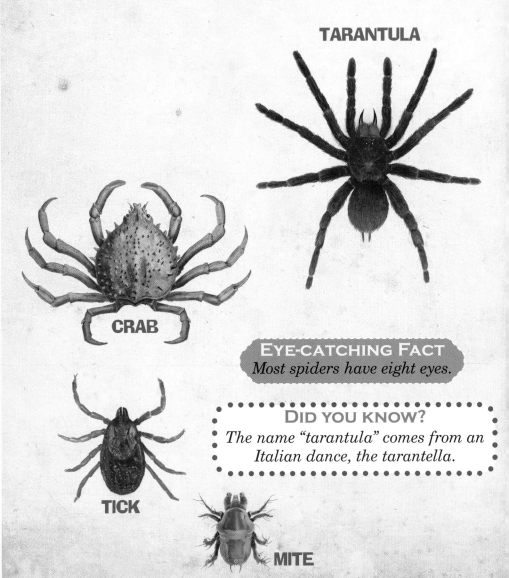

TARANTULA

CRAB

EYE-CATCHING FACT
Most spiders have eight eyes.

DID YOU KNOW?
The name "tarantula" comes from an Italian dance, the tarantella.

TICK

MITE

ALL IN THE FAMILY

You could say that a scorpion is a "land lobster."

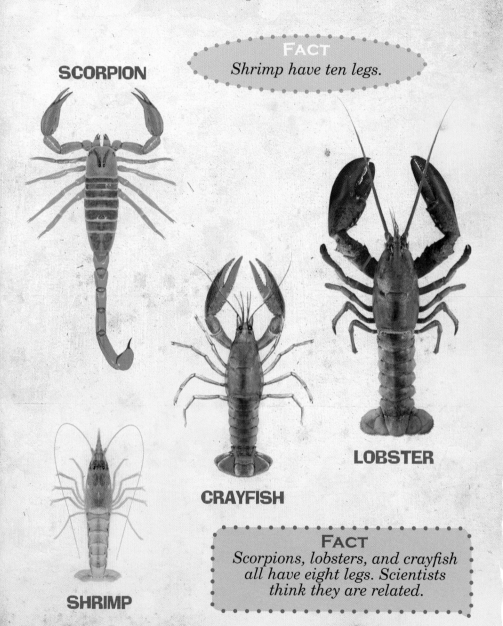

SCORPION

> ## FACT
> *Shrimp have ten legs.*

LOBSTER

CRAYFISH

SHRIMP

> ## FACT
> *Scorpions, lobsters, and crayfish all have eight legs. Scientists think they are related.*

YUMMY

Tarantulas are not vegetarians. They are carnivores. Tarantulas hunt and eat insects, other arachnids, tiny mice, lizards, snakes, and small birds.

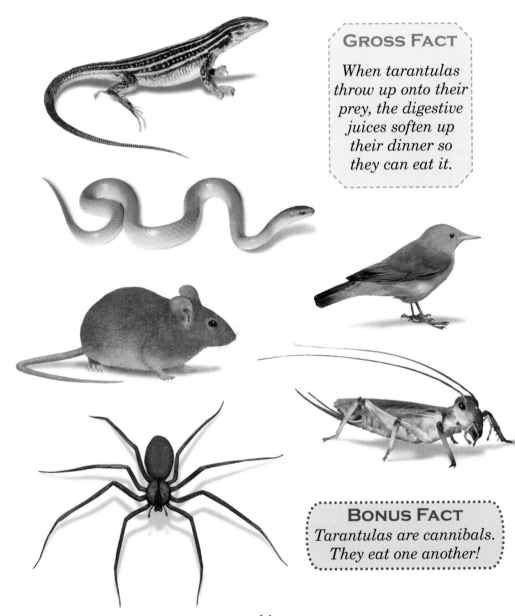

GROSS FACT

When tarantulas throw up onto their prey, the digestive juices soften up their dinner so they can eat it.

BONUS FACT
Tarantulas are cannibals. They eat one another!

DELICIOUS

Scorpions are not hunters. They wait for food to come to them. Scorpions mostly eat insects, spiders, and other bugs.

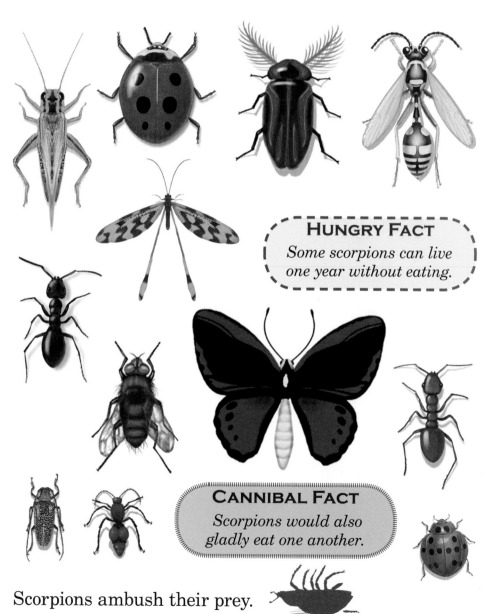

HUNGRY FACT

Some scorpions can live one year without eating.

CANNIBAL FACT

Scorpions would also gladly eat one another.

Scorpions ambush their prey.

MOLTING

Humans and other mammals have bones inside their bodies. Tarantulas and other arachnids have their skeletons on the outside of their bodies.

FACT
Tarantulas have an exoskeleton. An exoskeleton is an exterior shell.

To grow larger, the tarantula sheds its exoskeleton. This is called molting.

FACT
Mammals have an endoskeleton.

DID YOU KNOW?
When tarantulas molt, they shed their entire skin, including the linings of their mouth, respiratory organs, and stomach.

WE MOLT, TOO

Scorpions also have an exoskeleton. You could say that scorpions climb right out of their own skins.

> **FACT**
> *Scorpions are vulnerable when they shed their "shell."*

This is not a picture of two scorpions. On the left is the scorpion's old shell. On the right is the same scorpion with his new exoskeleton.

QUESTION
How can you tell which is the shell?

ANSWER
The one without eyes!

TASTY!

Some people eat tarantulas. They roast them over a fire on a stick and eat them like you would eat a marshmallow. Tarantulas are said to be delicious.

This is a bowl of roasted tarantulas. People in Asia, Africa, and South America enjoy eating them.

QUESTION
Do you think your school cafeteria should serve tarantulas for lunch?

DID YOU KNOW?
People from the Amazon rain forest squish the guts out of the abdomen and cook it like scrambled eggs.

BETTER THAN A HOT DOG?

Humans also eat scorpions. And not just a few people. Millions of people eat scorpions!

Which would you prefer? Scorpions on noodles? Or scorpions on rice and beans? Maybe for dessert you can lick a scorpion lollipop.

FACT
People in China eat millions of tons of scorpions per year.

DREAM THIS

This is a tarantula in attack mode. If you were ant-sized, this is what it would look like if you were fighting a tarantula.

> **FACT**
> *Eight legs give creatures great balance.*

THE TARANTULAS

The Tarantulas would be a great name for a football team.

IMAGINE THAT

The scorpion has a three-pronged attack — left claw, right claw, and a piercing tail. Pretend you are fighting a giant scorpion. It would look like this!

BIG ANCIENT FACT
A fossil of an eight-foot-long sea scorpion was recently discovered.

THE SCORPIONS

The Scorpions would be a cool name for a baseball team.

YOUNG TARANTULAS

A mother tarantula does not take care of her young. As soon as the spiderlings are born, they are on their own.

SCORPION BABIES

Scorpions are good mothers. They carry their cute little babies on their backs.

FUN FACT
Scorpions have been on Earth for more than 400 million years.

INTERESTING FACT
Scorpions have been on Earth longer than spiders.

QUESTION
Do you think a baby scorpion is called a scorpling or a baby scorpion?

ANSWER
A baby scorpion is called a scorpling.

THINGS TARANTULAS FIND DIFFICULT

*Finding glasses
with eight lenses.*

*Finding matching
shoes.*

*Finding a hairdresser
that won't run away.*

PLACES YOU DON'T WANT TO FIND A SCORPION

On your face while you've been sleeping.

Near the bathroom.

In your lunch box.

The tarantula is climbing a tree. The tips of its legs are like little needles. It has no trouble climbing.

The scorpion, as usual, is hidden under a rock. It doesn't want to bother anyone. It is waiting for some food to walk by.

Soon it is dusk. The scorpion takes a peek outside.

The scorpion gets a surprise! The tarantula jumps on top of it. Normally the tarantula would use its legs and palps to pin down an insect and jab it with its mouth fangs. But the scorpion fights back. The tarantula does not like the snapping scorpion claws.

The scorpion scrambles and escapes.

The scorpion uses its claws and tail to fight. It backs off, then runs right at the tarantula. It grabs the tarantula's palps with its claws, then jabs one of its legs. The scorpion shoots venom into the tarantula's leg.

The tarantula is bigger than the scorpion, but now one of its legs is numb. The tarantula flips the scorpion over, but the scorpion gets right back up and jabs another leg.

While the tarantula wonders what's wrong with its legs, the scorpion jabs it in the body.

The poison starts working, and the tarantula eventually stops moving. The scorpion will eat the tarantula.

WHO HAS THE ADVANTAGE? CHECKLIST

TARANTULA		SCORPION
☐	Size	☐
☐	Home	☐
☐	Claws	☐
☐	Stinger	☐
☐	Fangs	☐
☐	Hunting style	☐

Author note: This is one way the fight might have ended.
How would you write the ending?